My Little CREATIVE CRAYON

PETER PAUPER PRESS, INC.
Rye Brook, New York

PETER PAUPER PRESS

In 1928, at the age of twenty-two, Peter Beilenson began printing books on a small press in the basement of his parents' home in Larchmont, New York. Peter—and later, his wife, Edna—sought to create fine books that sold at "prices even a pauper could afford."

Today, still family owned and operated, Peter Pauper Press continues to honor our founders' legacy of quality, value, and fun for big kids and small kids alike.

Written by Hannah Beilenson
Designed by Heather Zschock

3 International Drive
Rye Brook, NY 10573 USA

Published in the UK and Europe by Peter Pauper Press, Inc.
c/o White Pebble International
Units 2-3, Spring Business Park
Stanbridge Road
Havant, Hampshire PO9 2GJ, UK

ISBN 978-1-4413-4209-6
Printed in China

7 6 5 4 3 2 1

Visit us at www.peterpauper.com

OUR ACTIONS AND US

Have you ever tried something new? Shared a toy or snack? Given a hug or high five when someone needed it? Well, those are just a few examples of putting your feelings into action! And every action you take can make a change. You can make people smile and laugh, help others feel safe, and create something new for everyone to share. There's so much you can do, and there's no wrong place to start—so let's take action today!

One action is **Creativity**, and we'll meet someone who will help us learn more about it.

I don't understand our homework.
Yeah, it says to do something creative? I don't get it.
That sounds like fun!

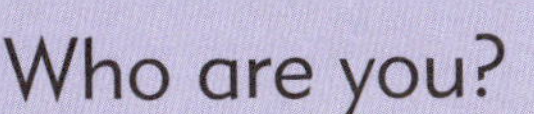

Who are you?

I'm a **Creative Crayon**! I help you practice creativity.

What's that?

Creativity is when you use your imagination to *create* something new.

So, when you draw,

or sing,
TALENT SHOW!

Once upon a time...
or write,

you're practicing creativity!
Oh, so it's when I make something?

Yes, but creativity isn't just about things you make—you can think creatively, too.

Asking questions,

reading,

and even just observing
the world around you

are also ways of being creative,
because you're using your imagination!
But what is
imagination?

It's when you picture something in your mind, even when it's not right in front of you.

And that can be really helpful, because it lets you see things in brand-new ways.

When you make a mistake and learn from it,

and when you encounter a problem but see it as an opportunity,

that's you using your imagination—you take what you see, and turn it into something new using your mind.

That's how people make great art,

and make the world a better place.
And we can do it, too?

You already have!
Just look
around you!

Meet My Creative Crayon

My Creative Crayon's name is:

....

When I'm creative, I like to make:

....

....

....

I use my imagination when:

....

....

....

....